Yorkshire, Quiet Places

by

FRANK MELLOR

Published by: Hendon Publishing Co. Ltd., Hendon Mill, Nelson, Lancs.
Text © Frank Mellor, 1973
First Edition June 1973
Second inpression June 1987
Printed by: Turner & Earnshaw Ltd., Westway House, Sycamore Avenue, Burnley, Lancashire.

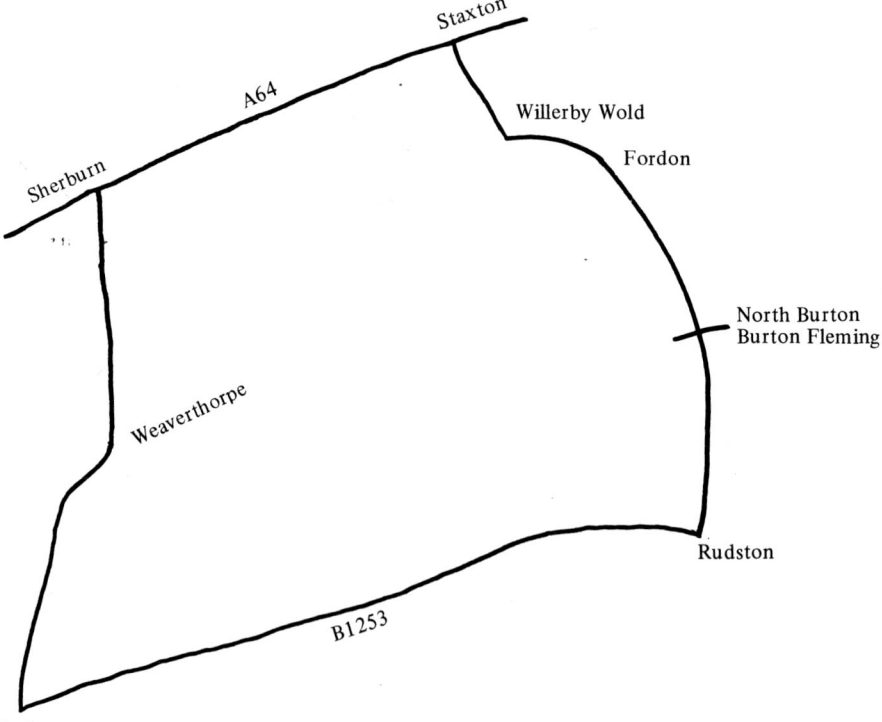

WEAVERTHORPE — SLEDMERE — RUDSTON

I have very vivid recollections of my first journey to Weaverthorpe fifty years ago. My father had a James motor cycle combination, I was on my mother's lap in the sidecar. Going down the long incline from the Wold top it hit a rough patch of road and overturned, the roads were not so well surfaced in those days. Mother was trapped and eventually my father got the thing on three wheels again but had to take mother to Malton to have her ring cut off her swelling finger. Her arm was badly bruised and swelling.

Another clear recollection of forty years ago was my cycle ride from Scarborough to Sledmere. I remember the Church and in particular the little quiet room with a selection of books, which I understand was a retreat for Sir Tatton Sykes.

Sledmere is still today a quiet retreat for a great many people. It is a great joy to visit. The Wolds are the finest agricultural areas in England, thanks to the Sykes of Sledmere.

From Scarborough take the A64 to Sherburn then turn south along an unclassified road signposted to Weaverthorpe. This leads through a gentle dale to the Wold top and then down the long south-facing run through undulating arable land to Weaverthorpe. The Church is on the left half a mile before you reach the village. Do stop and visit this church. I had passed it many times before I first stopped and went inside. Then I realised how indebted the Wold villages are to the second Sir Tatton Sykes who lavished £1,500,000 on the restoration and rebuilding of Wold churches. Weaverthorpe Church is beautiful inside.

All these Wold churches are worthy of attention irrespective of your religious belief. They are a wonderful testament to a great family who built up the wealth of the Wolds and gave a lot back to the people. This is Christian witness. They are quiet places where one can think and admire the craftsmanship and artistry in windows, architecture and carving. Not without humour also, at Sherburn the chancel screen has a variety of carvings and near the pulpit depicts a man yawning as though the sermon bores him. Thixendale, Fimber, Kirby Grindalythe and Langtoft are a few of the other lovely churches.

From the church, forward to the village which is small. Turn right through the village. The stream runs on your left and is quite an attraction for the children. I have always felt Weaverthorpe looked rather a poor village, the result I think of the hard times in the 30's, but in recent years it has improved.

We proceed about a mile along the road and then fork left signposted Sledmere. These are quiet country lanes through well farmed land. This countryside is a pleasure at all times of the year. In springtime the varying shades of green of fields of clover, wheat, barley and wheeling lapwing, in summer the swaying crops ripening, and later, gathered by squadrons of combines, the finest barley, often exported from Scarborough harbour for continental brewing. In autumn ploughing commences early accompanied by flocks of gulls.

Prior to 1771 this vast area was little more than a barren tract of sheep walks. Sir Christopher Sykes and his son Tatton over a period of thirty years transformed it into fertile land and set an example of agricultural management to the rest of the country.

Entering Sledmere turn right towards the church and leave the car underneath the beautiful group of beech trees. Opposite the church are two monuments. Temple Moore designed the copy of an Eleanor Cross which is a war memorial. The village well erected as a memorial to Sir Christopher Sykes is inscribed:-

"This edifice was erected by Sir Tatton Sykes, Bt., to the memory of his father Sir Christopher Sykes, Bt., who by assiduity and perseverance in building, planting and enclosing the Yorkshire Wolds, in the space of thirty years, set such an example to other owners of land as had caused what was once a blank and barren tract of country to become now one of the most productive and best cultivated districts in the County of York."

This is still true today. Sir Tatton Sykes laid the foundation of the famous Sledmere Stud. He had hundreds of horses and was a great character. He would join a workman breaking stones and work with him a while and talk, then continue his tour. He died in 1863 and was followed by the second Sir Tatton Sykes who developed the stud. His horses won classic races and often went to found other studs throughout the country.

From this memorial you can see several paddocks with bloodstock. I will always remember an interesting talk one afternoon with the blacksmith in Sledmere. He had just finished shoeing a shire-horse and lit a cigarette from a red hot iron drawn out of the forge. He told us how he went to the stables to shoe and would also watch horses at gallops and would make "orthopaedic" shoes to correct faulty gait. He could not get an apprentice to learn all this craft from him. He gave us a racing plate and I often think of this charming craftsman now gone and smithy demolished.

The smaller monument nearby is to the Wagoners. The son of the second Sir Tatton Sykes, who died in 1913 was Sir Mark Sykes who just before the First World War raised The Yorkshire Wagoners' Reserve. These men were used to horses and joined from all parts of the Wolds. When war broke out they became embodied in the Army Service Corps. I understand Sir Mark Sykes designed this memorial. The stone relief panels depict the soldiers enlisting, training, fighting and also illustrate their peacetime activities reaping, felling, and tending stock.

Now we must have a look at the church also designed by Temple Moore. It is a lovely church in a beautiful setting. There is an illuminated book of remembrance. A narrow stair leads up into the tiny room where the second Sir Tatton used to read his favourite books.

From the church we proceed to Sledmere House the home of Sir Tatton Sykes Bart., At certain times it is open to visitors - an opportunity not to be missed. A Georgian House, it was built in 1751 and enlarged by Sir Christopher Sykes in 1787. The layout of the 200 acre park was designed by Capability Brown who first cleared the old village and rebuilt it away from the mansion as he did with Harewood when Harewood House was erected. The house was seriously damaged by fire in 1911 but even the original moulds were used to restore the plasterwork which was by Joseph Rose in the Adam style. It contains Chippendale, Sheraton and French furniture, porcelain and statuary. The library is 100 feet long and comparable with the finest in the country.

The Turkish Room is a copy of a Sultan's apartment and was added by Sir Mark Sykes, who had great knowledge of and service in the Middle East. The first time I visited Sledmere House it was opened to raise Red Cross Funds and I shall always remember a huge glass tank filled with lilies on the top of the grand piano. How many I do not know, possibly fifty, the perfection of display and perfume was beautiful.

Sledmere has a classical atmosphere of that period of architecture and living I call the Grand Manner. The atmosphere of 200 years ago is still there, the finest of architecture, planning, literary taste, agricultural development, bloodstock breeding, paintings, and music. It is an experience to visit Sledmere House, very much a home.

I think I have whetted your appetite for a visit to Sledmere, without telling you more. We have an appetite too for tea which we can have at Sledmere House before we leave on the B 1253 Bridlington road making our way to Rudston which is on the old Roman way from Bridlington to York.

It was there that in 1933 a ploughman brought to light a wonderful tiled floor of a Roman Villa. These were carefully transferred in 1963 by Sir Mortimer Wheeler to the Transport Museum at Hull. I can thoroughly recommend a day's visit there to see this reconstructed villa floor and the other exhibits and at the same time visit Wilberforce House, the home of William Wilberforce who ended the slave trade, I must tell you more of this another time.

Rudston has a strange 25ft. monolith in the churchyard. It has been described as a bolt fired at the church by Satan. Some declare it to be prehistoric. I suppose we may call it the Rud Stone.

Winifred Holtby was born in Rudston on 23 June 1898 and the Wolds are the setting for her stories, "South Riding", "Land of Green Ginger" and "Pavements at Anderby". To her friend she wrote about Rudston - "Part of me seems to fit into their hills and hollows as one does in a familiar and well hollowed bed". She was educated in Scarborough. A great champion for peace and black Africa, unfortunately she only lived thirty-seven years and was buried in Rudston churchyard.

"God give me work till my life shall end
And life till my work is done."

I think we can compare Winifred Holtby and the Wolds with the Brontes and Haworth.

From Rudston we turn North to North Burton or Burton Fleming, then Fordon and Willerby Wold over rich farm land to Staxton with the magnificent panorama view over the vale, the North York Moors rising in the far distance, Oliver's Mount and Scarborough to the north east. A view I always stop and admire. Now home, having thoroughly enjoyed the quiet serenity of the Wolds.

The Monolith — All Saints, Rudston
Pre Historic

Weaverthorpe Church — Built in honour of St. Andrew, 1110
Restored 1872

Sledmere House — Georgian, 1751
Enlarged 1787

First World War Waggoners' Memorial
Designed by Sir Mark Sykes

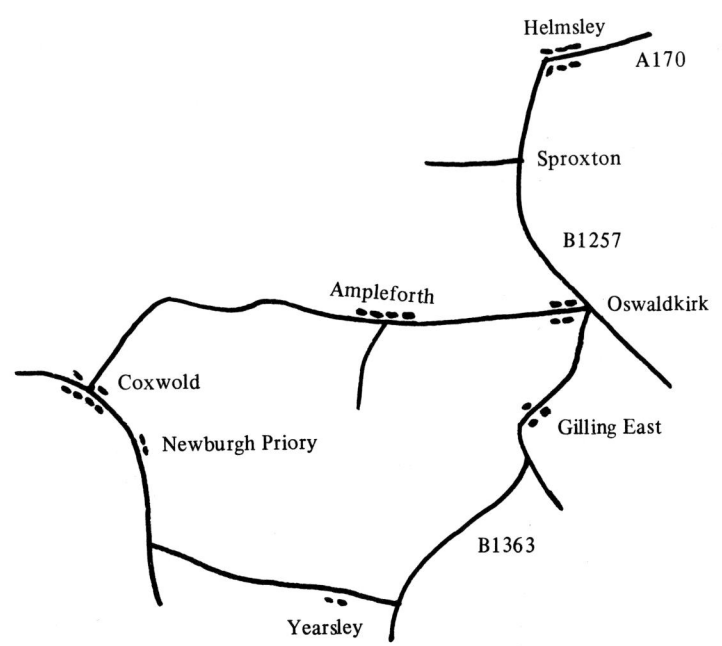

AMPLEFORTH, COXWOLD & GILLING EAST

The North York Moors National Park contains a wide variety of country and coast, some very rugged beauty, also some sheltered havens. Today we will relax in quiet places on the southern boundary of the national park in delightful villages very sheltered by the Hambledon Hills and extensive moors to the north.

The A170 passes through Helmsley and after a few miles we take the B1257 signposted Malton, passing through Sproxton, with a charming tiny church of St. Chad, to Oswaldkirk, which has a very fine Norman Church. Here we turn right to Ampleforth.

Between Oswaldkirk and Ampleforth lies Ampleforth College. It is an outstanding Roman Catholic Public School and also the great modern Benedictine Abbey of St. Laurence. The Benedictine Order was founded in 529 by St. Benedict. In 1793 the Honourable Ann Fairfax of Gilling Castle built a house at Ampleforth for her chaplain Fr. Anselm Bolton and in 1802 a community of English Benedictines settled there.

This Benedictine foundation traces its origin to St. Edward the Confessor and the community at Westminster Abbey before the dissolution of the monastery. At the dissolution they fled to France, and at the time of the French Revolution they had again to seek refuge and so in 1802 they found a permanent home in Ampleforth. From the beginning they ran a school, and development from that day has been outstanding.

The monastery was built in 1893. In 1899 St. Laurence Priory was raised to the status of an Abbey. The Abbey Church was designed by Sir Giles Gilbert Scott and was started in 1924 and was opened in 1961.

When we visited Ampleforth we were kindly invited to visit the Abbey Church. The monks were holding a service which was nearly finished, so we waited, but were able to hear some of the chants, which were most impressive. The unusual feature of the church is the central altar between choir and nave.

Four arches support the great dome. There are beautiful carvings of foliage with animals, fox, squirrel, birds and I understand that the masons let the boys watch them carve and let them choose the subjects. This is an example of free expression in the true tradition of craftsmanship. There is an altar stone from Byland Abbey. The woodwork was carved by Robert Thompson of Kilburn, his mark the mouse carved on each piece. The whole church is of great beauty, one cannot fail to kneel in prayer and give thanks for the devotion and inspiration of this Benedictine Order for its work in education, agriculture, craftsmanship, and art.

There is a very fine modern library at the College with a rich collection of books, some from the 15th and 16th century, again furnished in oak by Robert Thompson. The College has nearly 700 scholars, with extensive playing fields and farms.

We left the Abbey Church feeling very thankful that the traditions of this ancient Benedictine Order were being applied to our youth today.

The village of Ampleforth lies a little to the west and has a number of interesting features. St. Hilda's church was rebuilt in 1868, a few ancient items have been preserved, a Norman south door and arch in the nave.

If you like a stiff walk and are interested in antiquities, just out of the village a path goes North climbing above 750 feet to Studford Ring, an ancient encampment from the Bronze Age, and just a few hundred yards beyond there is a deep ditch called Double Dykes and a number of tumuli. The extensive views from here are ample reward for the climb. For those who prefer a gentle walk Ampleforth is a pleasant little village to wander round and admire.

Then we proceed to Coxwold which I think is one of the gems of Yorkshire and still not overwhelmed with cars. It nestles between the Hambledon and Howardian Hills, stone cottages on either side of a broad green gently rising up to the church.

On the left there is an interesting range of almhouses dating from the days of Charles II (1662). I think these are excellent examples of architecture and very relevant to today's needs for the elderly. Opposite is the Faucenberg Arms, a first-class old English inn but first I think we will see the rest of the village and then return for a drink and a meal.

On the same side further up the street is Shandy Hall where the novelist and 18th century wit Laurence Sterne resided from 1760 to 1768. Here he completed "Tristram Shandy" and wrote "Sentimental Journey". He was the eccentric parson to the village. Shandy Hall is a quaint old brick house, very neglected at one time, but it has now been restored and maintained as a building of architectural and historical significance.

The old Grammar School was founded in 1603 by Sir John Hart. He was a local boy and became Lord Mayor of London. The property is now a private residence. Beyond this is Colville Hall, a Tudor House.

The dominating feature of the village at the crest of the hill is the very fine 15th century church of St. Michael. In 757 Pope Paul I wrote to Eadbert King of Northumbria calling on him to restore the monasteries of Stonegrave, Coxwold and Jarrow. The church has an unusual octagonal tower. A copy of the Geneva Bible printed in 1601 is in a case carved by Robert Thompson of Kilburn and again you will see the mouse mark. The nave windows contain 15th century glass. There is a brass inscription to John Manston (1464) on the floor of the nave. The three-decker pulpit is unique. There are many monuments to the Belasyse family. Anthony Belasyse was one of the Commissioners for the Dissolution of the Monasteries and Henry VIII granted him Newburgh Priory which is nearby. There is a monument in marble of Thomas, Earl of Fauconberg, who married Mary Cromwell, the daughter of Oliver Cromwell. She is reputed to have brought her father's body from London and secretly interred it at Newburgh Priory, but more of that very soon. The church is full of history, the whole village is of great interest but now it is time to take refreshment at the Fauconberg Arms.

After lunch and before sitting in the car again, walk down the village to the potter's studio which is on the right at the end of the village. Here is an excellent craftsman his pieces going all over the world pleasant reminders of Coxwold.

A little way beyond Coxwold is Newburgh Priory set in a lovely park with a lake. This is beautiful at all times of the year, and I remember my first visit was one sunny day in February and there were masses of snowdrops. The Priory was founded in 1145 by Roger de Mowbray and housed Augustinian Canons. One of the Canons, William Newburgh (1136-1198) was a great historian of the Norman Conquest to his own time.

Anthony Belasyse was given the Priory at the dissolution. Only traces of the old priory remain, additions have created a beautiful house.

Charles I created a Belasyse Baron Fauconberg, his son supported Cromwell and married his daughter Mary. Charles II had the bodies of Cromwell and Admiral Blake taken up from Westminster Abbey. Cromwell's body was hung up at Tyburn. The head was cut off and it is believed that Mary secretly obtained Cromwell's body and brought it to Newburgh Priory and sealed it up in the attic. This bricked-up portion has never been opened. I understand Cromwell's head is at Westminster Abbey – grim history!

The house and grounds are very peaceful today, one of our great historical treasures.

Moving on in an almost anti-clockwise circle we come to Gilling East, a charming village with stream running through and little bridges. The church of the Holy Cross is a mixture of styles, the tower is perpendicular. It contains many monuments to the Fairfax family, to Sir Nicholas Fairfax (1572) and to a 14th century Knight. Also memorials to rectors with links with Trinity College, Cambridge, patron of the living. The great Indian Cricketer Prince Ranjitsinghi used to visit Gilling; his tutor at Cambridge became rector here and the Prince often came to see him and play cricket. He gave the clock in the church tower.

On the hillside above the village is Gilling Castle which now belongs to Ampleforth College. This may be visited, the ancestral home of the Fairfax family. The basement is 14th century but the upper part is 18th century, thought to have been designed by Sir John Vanbrugh.

Sir William Fairfax built the Elizabethan dining room. This unique room was dismantled and sold to an American a number of years ago but fortunately it has since been recovered and restored. The Great Chamber of panelled walls and stained glass is considered to be one of the most beautiful and complete specimens of Elizabethan design.

Gilling Castle has a wonderful position, beautiful grounds and terraced garden, the Hambledon Hills to the North and the Howardian Hills to the South. This geological fault is called the "Gilling Gap". The Castle must have held a strategic position.

When we visited it the gardens were beautiful. Peaches and figs were ripening on the terrace walls, the herbacious borders were at their best, the views all round showed the countryside in full summer and as we returned to the car the huntsman was exercising the pack of Ampleforth beagles.

We finish our return journey on the B1363 back to Oswaldkirk again joining the B1257 having gone full circle we return via A170.

I consider this to be an outstanding day out in full rich country. Rich in so many ways, architecturally, historically and intellectually. As we started in the company of Benedictine Monks at Ampleforth College, so we leave them at Gilling Castle. A very memorable day.

Coxwold — Village

Coxwold — Fauconberg Hospital, 1662

Coxwold – Shandy Hall

Coxwold – St. Michael's Church

Newburgh Priory

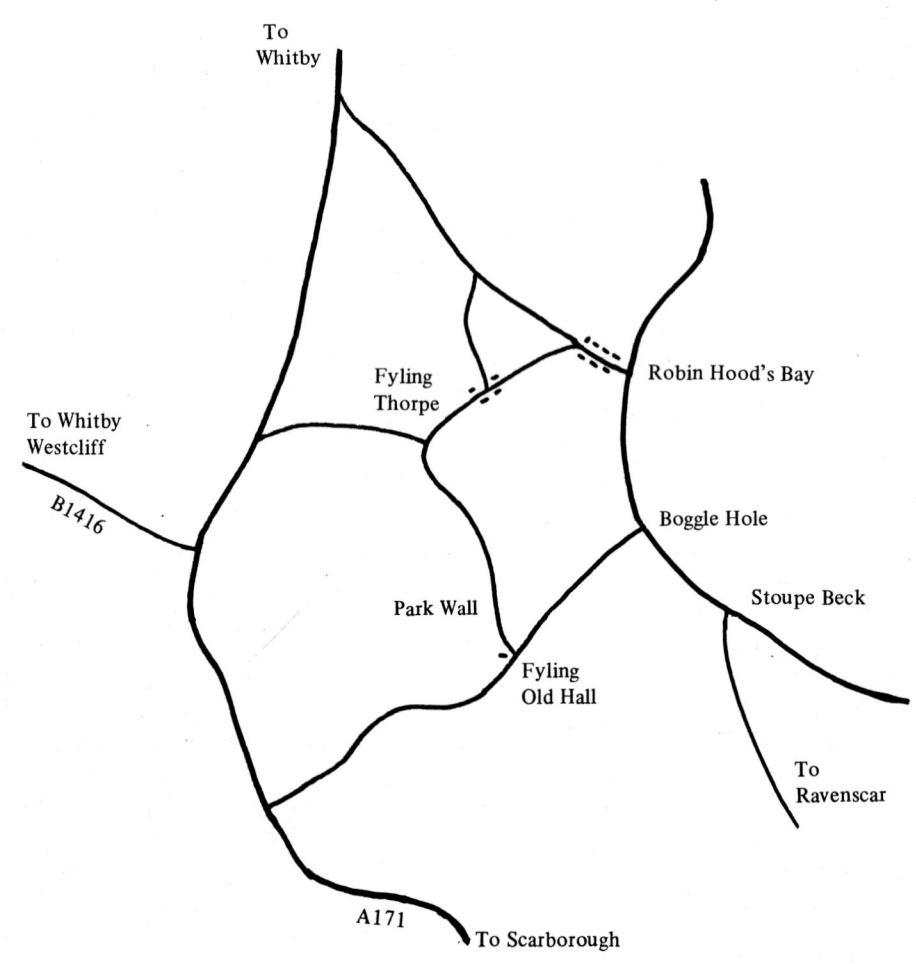

ROBIN HOOD'S BAY.

    Early in the summer we visited Ravenscar and walked along to Robin Hood's Bay, but the tide did not permit us to explore "The Bay" and it is such a charming place we have planned a special visit timed with the tide. The greatest pleasure is derived from a visit to "The Bay" when the tide is out so we looked up the times of high tide which happened to be 6.10am/6.21pm. Tides at this time are near maximum and when the tide goes out it exposes the shore, so that one can plan to take a snack lunch on to the rocks and take full advantage of the day.
    It is a very rugged outlook over the moors on the A171, very little changed from pre-historic times. Looking at the Ordnance Survey Sheet, there are many tumuli and earthworks marked, showing that there were many settlements. The early Bronze Age folk built stone circles, the best known being Stonehenge, approximately dated 1600-1000BC. We pass a stone circle on our left just beyond the Harewood Dale road, called Standing Stones Rigg.
There was probably a burial chamber in the centre; four cup and ring marked rocks are in Scarborough Museum from this site. Again, opposite the junction of the B1416 road to Whitby West Cliff the ordnance sheet marks standing stones and further over to the east is marked "Park Wall". This is where the Abbot of Whitby had his deer park in 1404 and the monks had a mill and lime kiln at Fylingdales.
    I often approach Robin Hood's Bay from Fyling Hall and I well remember cycling this way in my teenage days and having to carry my cycle over Stoupe Beck to join the track to Ravenscar. What a climb up to the Peak, but what a glorious thrill the ride down from Ravenscar towards Scarborough with that magnificent view of Hayburn Wyke, Scarborough Castle, Filey Brigg and Flamborough nearly 30 miles in the far distance. But back to the history.
    The Romans had a signal station at Ravenscar until about AD 395. The area was raided by Vikings who destroyed the Monastery of St. Hilda at Whitby in 867. The Vikings were described as daring, adventurous, powerful and dangerous, and as I see the history of Robin Hood's Bay they must have been the stock of the hardy fishermen.

Fyling is mentioned in Domesday and Robin Hood's Bay was described by King Henry VIII's topographer Leland in 1536. There is in Rotterdam's Prince Hendrick's Maritime Museum a chart by Waghenaer of 1586 describing the coast of Europe. "Robinhoodes Bay" is marked with a compass course from Rotterdam 275 miles. In those times it must have been quite an important place to shipping.

So through Fyling Thorpe we make our way to Robin Hood's Bay and park the car at the top of "The Bank". I have a very old Ward Lock guide of Scarborough and District which states that at Fyling, bold Robin Hood is supposed to have hid when he waylaid the servants of the Abbot of Whitby as they passed along the great causeway which then led to Hackness. Other stories say that he sought refuge at the Bay and that he helped the Abbot of Whitby to repel sea pirates. The origin of the name remains a mystery, and as we walk down to the sea through this quaint and fascinating village there remains an air of mystery, it is all part of the atmosphere of the place.

All so curiously built in a higgledy-piggledy way yet easily explained. Most of these old buildings were on 1000 year leases and instead of young couples moving away from home it was customary for mother and daughter to remain under one roof as long as the number permitted. When increasing accommodation became necessary the old folks preferred sacrificing a little yard or garden upon which a small cottage could be put up. So the wives could retain the companionship which was so helpful during the long sea voyages of the breadwinners. They shared the little wash kitchens, often one or two of the children slept with Granny. In days past this was an extremely close-knit community.

At one time this Bay was one of the largest fishing centres on the North East Coast, the men fishing the North Sea and sailing the oceans of the World. As many as 173 ships of sail were owned by the inhabitants, generally in shares of fourths and eighths. Syndicates were formed, mutual insurance was organised. Many embarked on whaling ventures and many of the male population over fourteen would be away for nine months of the year.

Their cobles had a very striking resemblance to the Norwegian fishing craft, suitable for landing upon open beaches. Fish would be dried and smoked as the Norwegians do. Their names and speech bore resemblances, too.

The life of the fisherfolk has been beautifully recorded in photographs by Frank Sutcliffe of Whitby: the cobbles, fishermen in thigh boots and sou'westers, the wives in shawls and bonnets, the old men with weather-beaten faces. Leo Walmsley wrote vividly of life in the Bay called Bramblewick in his novels "Sally Lunn" and "Three Fevers", filmed as "Turn of the Tide". Now the cottages are taken for holidays and the boat landing by sailing dinghies.

In the 18th century smuggling or "free trade" played quite an important part in the life of the Bay. Tea was heavily taxed and cost 20/- to 30/- a lb; in Holland it was under 1/- lb. Rum, Brandy, Gin, Tobacco and Silk all yielded rich rewards. The fishermen of the Bay linked with the continental ports and the people in the Bay could land it quickly and quietly and distribute it as easily as they distributed their fish. The houses, being built upon one another, could hide contraband and pass it from one to another through cupboards.

In 1808 the laws were tightened, despite the protests of the boatmasters and fishermen of the Bay on the grounds that these laws would affect their herring fishing! The steam cutter, and heavy penalties made the risks too great, but even in 1830 the Dragoons were stationed in the Bay. There are many reports in the Military and Customs records of these smuggling activities.

As we wander down the Bank one can imagine the intriguing history of the Bay: fishing, whaling, smuggling; the changes wrought by steam as it replaced wooden sailing ships. The man who once sailed the world had to leave never to return.

Now the summer visitors bring trade in curios and a few crafts like the potter Roma Hodgson. The **marine life of the Bay is now for leisure and academic studies.** The building on the right at the foot of the Bank used to be the Marine Laboratory of Leeds University, but has now been closed. We walk down the slipway and see the expanse of rock and bay. The tide is out and so we go and explore this marvellous bay. The very names of the rocks are fascinating, from north to south, Dungeon Hole, West Scar, Ground Wyke Hole, Landing Scar, East Scar and most charming Dab Dumps. The reefs run out to sea in a series of rocky **ledges of great geological interest.**

Here we sit on one of the ledges facing the sun and have our picnic lunch with the view of The Peak at Ravenscar before us.

Whilst the tide is at its lowest, the children enjoy searching for crabs, eels and sea urchins. As the tide turns it is pleasant to have a walk along the sand between the cliff and rocks. There are lots of fossils, many ammonites (a round coil). The abundance of ammonites and the great variety of their shape and ornament resulted in their use as a method of subdivision of the lias. This series of beds was subdivided in zones and later into sub-zones, the thinnest division being only a few feet thick, yet each characterised by the presence of a distinctive ammonite. The ammonite was used in the crest of Whitby Abbey in the fourteenth century.
    It is not far to walk on to Boggle Hole where the mill used to be, now a youth hostel. Here you can return via the cliff walk which is part of the Cleveland Way. Along this walk we pass Farside House (1680) on our left. The Farsides came from Farside Castle, Midlothian. John Farside was bow bearer and ranger to the Forest of Pickering appointed by James I. There is a beautiful brass plaque in Scalby Church to an Adam Farside and a charity in his name, perhaps the families were connected. Past Cowfield Hill we return into the Bay and enjoy a cup of tea before wandering through the narrow alleys back up to the car park. It is more interesting and less tiring this way. Sometimes there is an exhibition of paintings by local artists. You can relax in so many ways here. Rather reluctantly we climb back into the car and away through Thorpe Green, Park Gate and Brow Top on to the moor again with distant views out to the North Sea.

Robin Hood's Bay — Quaint Cottages

Robin Hood's Bay — The Bolts

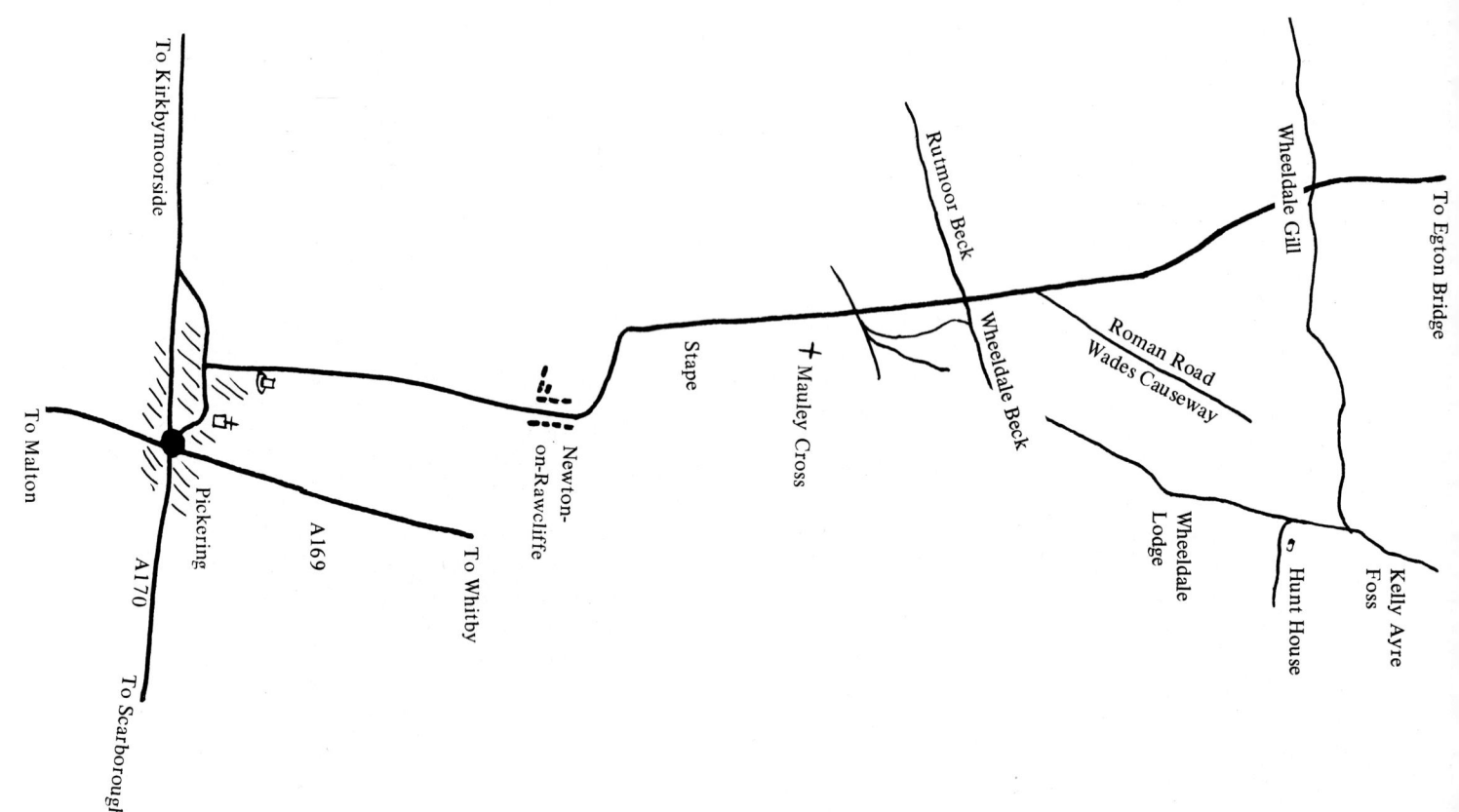

PICKERING & WADE'S CAUSEWAY.

   Today our visit takes us to a very familiar place and to a remote part of the moor almost as it was 2000 years ago. Very often we are so familiar with places near to us we do not pay sufficient attention to them or take interest in them and I think this is so with Pickering. People tend to go along the A170 and miss the most interesting part of this ancient market town.
   As we enter Pickering the sign with the Coat of Arms describes the town "Gateway to the Moors founded 270B.C." The Coat of Arms is surmounted by a pike with a ring in its mouth. It was called PICKERINGA in XIIIth century writings. Older chroniclers claim that King Peredurus was the son of Morindus who was devoured by a monster. The young King Peredurus lost a ring and accused a maiden of stealing it. But his cook found it in the stomach of a pike caught in the River Costa. The King, out of remorse at the false accusation, married the maiden and named the Town "Pike-ring". This makes a charming start to our visit. The ancient history of the town is certainly authenticated by the Neolithic, Bronze and Iron Age remains which have been found. It was described as a borough in 1206-7 but this status disappeared in 1894 when it became an Urban District.
   Only thirty minutes from Scarborough at the traffic island where the roads Whitby/Malton intersect the Scarborough/Kirkbymoorside take the right fork up "Shiddy Hill" as it is called and park in the market place. The old stone buildings with pantilex roofs are quite picturesque. First we visit the Parish Church of St. Peter and St. Paul with fine tower and steeple. The columns are 12th century and the clerestory in 15th century. On these walls are famous murals painted in the 15th century, at one time covered with whitewash and accidentally discovered in 1851. They portray St. George fighting the dragon, St. Christopher, the Martyrdom of St. Edmund, the murder of Thomas à Becket, Herod's Feast, a series of eleven scenes representing the history of St. Catherine of Alexandria, the seven acts of mercy and others. There are memorials to Robert and Nicholas King, Pickering men who surveyed Washington, of particular interest to visiting Americans. The Pulpit is outstanding, described as Hepplewhite and by another as Chippendale.
   There is a memorial to William Marshall, a great agriculturalist, also lovely Georgian candelabra. The

town's medieval woolmen obviously gave well to their church. The wealth of Pickering today is centred on a broad based agriculture, sheep, dairy, pigs, poultry, barley, nurseries and forestry.

From the Church we turn at the corner shop up Burgate and Castlegate to the Castle. This is a very fine example of motte and bailey type of fortress and dating from William the Conqueror's time, at first earthworks and timber, stonework from about 1100. There are many records of the Kings of England visiting this castle between 1100 and 1400, hunting deer and wild boar in the Forest of Pickering. Henry I dated a charter there in 1122, Henry II visited it and gave a charter there to the weavers of York. The Court of King John was held there in 1201. Edward I was there 25th September 1280 and August 26-29th 1292. Edward II commanded the present outer walls and tower to be erected and intended it to be a permanent Royal Castle, but he was deposed in 1325, when it was handed to Henry, younger brother of Earl Thomas of Lancaster. Edward III visited in 1334 and Richard II was imprisoned there in 1399 before he was murdered at Pontefract. From this commanding position we look across the surrounding country with extensive views. Not far distant the defence of the realm is now centred at the Fylingdale Ballistic Missile Early Warning Station, which benefits the town of Pickering economically.

The 15th century Bell from the Castle Chapel I understand is in the Victoria and Albert Museum.

As we leave the Castle this reminds me of Pickering's own Museum and Art Centre at Beck Isle, a fine old house where William Marshall lived. I hope some day the Council will endeavour to make an interesting feature of the Keld Head Spring, the source of the River Costa. A little care and attention here would improve the passing impression one gets of Pickering.

Today we continue our relaxation by taking the road which runs parallel with the old railway line and Pickering Beck up to Newton upon Rawcliffe with extensive views over the Vale of Pickering to the Wolds beyond. The White Horse Inn dispenses hospitality. We proceed northwards and follow the road signposted Stape, a tiny hamlet which proudly presents the Stape Silver Band which so often gives us pleasure at some of the Agricultural Shows.

We pass the Mauley Cross on our right, and as the condition of the road deteriorates, don't be dismayed - it dips down to a little gill where we have often picnicked, watching the dragonflies, the wagtail and listening to the curlew. Further along, the road improves and drops to a lovely moorland valley with Wheeldale Beck running through. Stop here and leave the car, walk a little way up the hill. Here we visit the Roman Road, Wade's Causeway. The moors here are very little different from their appearance in Roman Times.

The first published record of Wade's Causeway is in Warburton's Map of Yorkshire which was engraved and supplied to subscribers in 1720. Warburton made new surveys and his marking of Roman roads was very valuable. The Scarborough and District Archaeological Society made a very complete research and report on this Roman road in 1964 for those who may become interested in a detailed study. It is concluded that Wade's Causeway was built as a military project about AD 80 and was used to about AD 120. It was part of the road from Derventio (now Malton) to Cawthorn, Lease Rigg and north possibly to the signal station at Goldsborough. The Roman surveyors certainly had great skill in planning the routes of their roads. This causeway is a good example of the way that they found the lowest practical crossing place of the moors at a height of 825 feet near Mauley Cross. No modern road makes a North/South crossing at a lower level.

The remains of this road today show how extremely well their roads were constructed, foundations of gravel and subsoil embanked and cambered to ensure drainage, then sandstone slabs with kerbstones set on edge to prevent spread, just the same principle as is applied in a modern road, in all about 18 feet wide, gravel and small stones spread on the surface, all drains by ditches and culverts.

Legend has it that Wade the Giant built the causeway for the convenience of his wife Bel who kept her cattle on the moors. They were both giants and are said to have built castles at Mulgrave and Pickering together, using one hammer between them, slinging it to and fro when each wanted it. Wade is mentioned in Chaucer's Merchant's Tale. From here there are some good walks to Wheeldale Lodge, Hunt House, Nelly Ayre Foss and attractive waterfall. The Wheeldale Beck flows on to Mallyan Spout, one can walk to Goathland and Beck Hole. The Lyke Wake Walk comes across this moor. You should have a map and compass and be sensible if you walk across these moors.

Have proper footwear and clothing. It is no place to lose your way and weather conditions can change very quickly. You can easily become a "Blue man i'-th'-Moss" as is marked on the Ordnance Survey near Wheeldale Howe at 1043 feet.

On the line of this old way towards Goathland is Julian Park. This area was granted by Henry III to Peter de Mauley in 1222. The stone we passed earlier in the day may have been a boundary mark. Peter de Mauley was living at Julian Park in 1294 when he granted land to Grosmont Priory. At this time Mulgrave Castle was being rebuilt.

Returning to the car proceed about a mile further to Wheeldale Gill. This is a lovely sheltered moorland valley and I am quite content to stay here and relax peacefully, though it is becoming better known as we all search for these quiet places.

From here we can return as we came or proceed over Egton High Moor through Grosmont with the pleasant views down the Esk Dale to Sleights. Or through Julian Park to Goathland. I prefer to return and enjoy the view over the Vale and Wolds and take refreshment at Newton or Pickering. The moorland air gives me an appetite and a pleasant drowsiness. Goathland, Beckhole and Egton Bridge are much too interesting to dash through, we will visit them on another day. Enough is as good as a feast and I think Pickering Church, its Castle and Wade's Causeway have been well worth our attention today, and the quiet atmosphere of Wheeldale Gill as soothing as vintage wine.

Mauley Cross — Stape

Wades Causeway — Roman Road

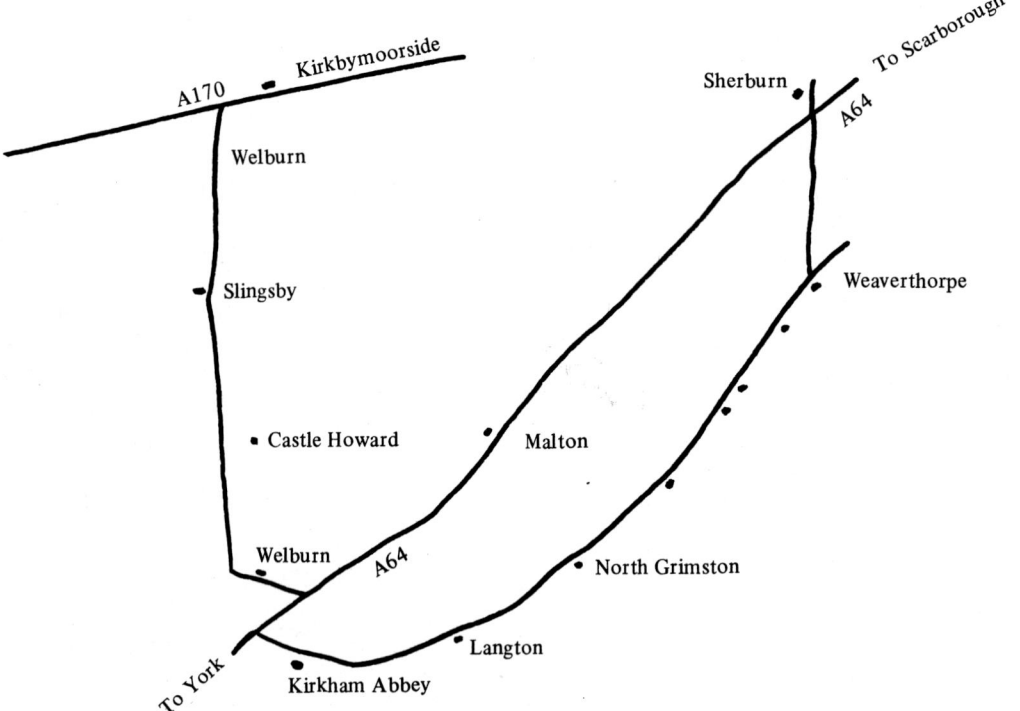

CASTLE HOWARD, KIRKHAM ABBEY, LANGTON

Prepare yourself for a sublime day, pack a basket with small glasses, a bottle of wine, fresh bread rolls, butter and cheese. I have enjoyed this circular tour very many times and taken visitors of many nationalities, I doubt if there are more interesting tours in the country. Along the A170 beyond Kirkbymoorside we turn left into Welburn. I chose this route years ago because it avoids traffic problems at Malton and takes a lovely quiet country lane through well farmed land. We pass over two fords over streams going into the Rye, through West Ness and East Ness on to Slingsby, a pleasant village of stone houses, red roofs, castle ruins and a church rebuilt in 1868, all sheltering at the foot of the Howardian Hills. We proceed forward crossing the Helmsley/Malton road B1257 and start to climb The road straightens out and soon before us is a road straight as a die for about four miles lined with beeches, an obelisk in the far distance. Soon we approach the Great Lake on the north side of Castle Howard. Here we stop and park the car and have a walk by the lake where we have seen heron and several kinds of water fowl. It is a delight for fishermen.

After the lakeside **walk we** return to the car and continue our drive to the obelisk, a **tribute** to Charles Howard, 3rd Earl of Carlisle, acting Earl Marshal of England whilst his cousin the Duke of Norfolk was a minor. He also became First Lord of the Treasury, this office is now held by the Prime Minister. The first time I saw this obelisk I was only in my teens and was exploring this area on a cycle, I can remember stopping to read the inscription and marvelled how the obelisk and beeches had stood the test of time since 1714. The plantations had certainly risen to perfection, pheasants strutted about beneath the beeches. Down the drive stands Castle Howard erected where the old castle of Henderskelfe stood which was burnt down in 1693.

This palace has been open to the public ever since it was first built and is equalled only by Blenheim Palace, the other of the two great palaces on which Vanbrugh and Hawksmoor worked together. Sir Christopher Wren was the pioneer of the English Baroque style of architecture and greatly influenced other architects of the time, especially Talman (who designed Chatsworth) and Hawksmoor and Vanbrugh.

Actually Talman was commissioned to design the 3rd Earl of Carlisle a house, but they had a dispute over fees and so parted company and the commission passed to Sir John Vanbrugh, a military man turned man of the theatre, now turned architect. He certainly applied his dramatic taste to architecture. Castle Howard was the first private residence to be built with a dome following Sir Christopher Wren's designs for St. Paul's and Greenwich.

Work started in 1701 and by 1714 Lord Carlisle was in residence, the centre, dome, south front, east wing and kitchens complete. Vanbrugh died in 1726 but Hawksmoor continued and designed his masterpiece, the Mausoleum. The West Wing was built between 1753 and 1759 to the design of Sir Thomas Robinson but it does not compare with Vanbrugh's dramatic style. The Stables were built between 1781-4 by John Carr of York. From the very outset the Howard Family have spent a vast fortune on the house and contents and all this time the public have had the pleasure of seeing and appreciating this glory of architecture and art.

Inside, the splendid proportions of the Great Hall and the whole of the interior are matched by the beautiful tapestries, paintings by Tintoretto, Rubens, Reynolds, Gainsborough, Holbein, and the most charming portrait by John Jackson of Lastingham, the little girl in blue, Lady Mary Howard later Lady Taunton; china in a wide range of Chelsea, Meissen and Crown Derby; furniture in many styles, Hepplewhite, Chippendale, Adam, French, and Chinese. The Guide Book details these and illustrates many beautifully. Books have also been compiled in recent years on the works of Vanbrugh and Hawksmoor, I have found these very interesting, covering a very fine period of English architecture and adding to the interest and appreciation of Castle Howard. It seems incredible that this palace was Vanbrugh's first essay in architecture.

After touring the house I like to walk out on to the south lawn and fountain to admire the south front. To the east lies Ray Wood and the Temple of the Four Winds again by Vanbrugh, whilst further in the distance is the Mausoleum which was designed by Hawksmoor. The 3rd Earl of Carlisle's body is interned in the Mausoleum, a man of noble spirit indeed to have undertaken this great adventure into architecture with Vanbrugh and Hawksmoor.

The Stables were built in 1781-4 and were designed by John Carr of York. They now form the Costume Galleries containing the largest private collection in Britain of 17th to 20th century dress.

There is a wealth of interest in Castle Howard and it is a place we can visit with pleasure many times. We leave, continuing the long drive from the Obelisk, through the Gate House arch.

We turn left through the second village of Welburn and then right on the A64 for about a mile and then left on the peaceful country lane again down to Kirkham Abbey. This was founded between 1122 and 1130 by Walter L'Espec, Lord of Helmsley. He also founded Rievaulx Abbey and Warden Abbey in Bedfordshire. Kirkham was an Augustinian house, this order was founded by St. Augustine of Hippo in the late 11th century. They wore a black cassock without a hood and a white surplice and were known as the Black Canons. They were all regular canons and lived in the priory but were at liberty to leave and take livings as parish priests.

Walter L'Espec's uncle William became first Prior. It was endowed with seven churches and rents from properties in Yorkshire and Northumberland and at one time was wealthy, but it must not have been well managed at all times for it was in debt at the beginning of the 14th century. At the Dissolution on 8th December 1538 it had only 16 resident canons and an income of £269.

It has a lovely setting on the East Riding bank of the River Derwent just above the weir. The best of the remains is the 13th century gatehouse. Carved in stone are the arms of de Rood, Scrope, de Fortibus, L'Espec, Vaux, de Clare, Fitz Ralph and England, also carvings of St. George and the Dragon and David and Goliath. A very fine fragment of this abbey is still left in the west wall of the cloister, two bays, here the monks washed their hands before going to their meal.

At the dissolution the estates of Howsham nearby were granted to the Bamburghs. The stone from the priory was used to build the mansion. Legend relates that because of this sacrilege the mansion was cursed and the male heirs doomed. The Bamburghs male line died out as did their successors, the Wentworths and then the Chomleys, strange coincidence! The priory was given to the nation by Lord Brotherton and is now maintained as an ancient monument, a place of quiet interest and relaxation.

From here we proceed to the Wolds and the charming village of Langton where we stop and sit on the village green and enjoy our cheese and wine refreshments.

At one end of the village is the church with ancient font and bells possibly pre-Reformation, there is a very touching memorial in the chancel to Mary Ingram who died in 1656. There are memorials to the Northcliffes who lived in the Hall at the other end of the village, the entrance gates are surmounted by greyhounds. Between Church and Hall the village green is flanked by stone cottages, many with uncommon lancet windows. Several years ago we stopped here and some village children had their rabbit feeding on the green, our children soon made friends and thoroughly enjoyed this interlude. Langton is quiet and unspoilt, being off the beaten track. Nearby are training stables and between Langton and Norton there is a training ground on Langton Wold.

We continue this wold way to North Grimston with its Norman Church, then through Kirby Grindalythe, West Lutton, Helperthorpe and Weaverthorpe. The churches here were all restored by G. E. Street for Sir Tatton Sykes.

At Weaverthorpe we turn left over Sherburn Wold and join the A64 Malton to Scarborough road home after a day in lovely countryside with the added pleasures of architectural and historic interests.

Castle Howard

Castle Howard – Fountain

Kirkham Abbey

Langton – Village

Langton – Village

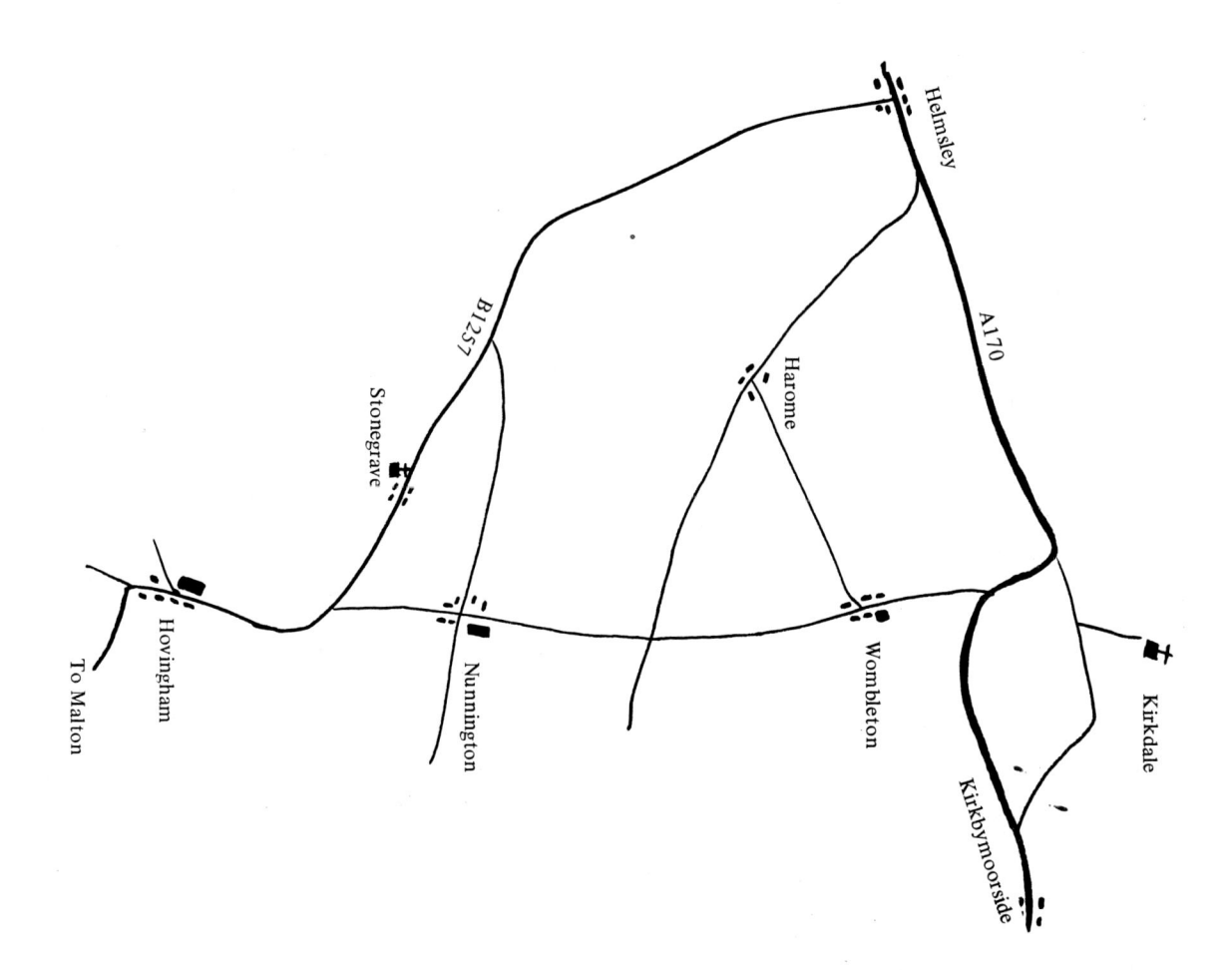

KIRKDALE - NUNNINGTON - HOVINGHAM.

This outing today takes us to lovely ancient sheltered churches and country mansions. On the A170 about half a mile out of Kirkbymoorside we turn right at the signpost to St. Gregory Minster. The road passes over a ford crossing the lovely Hodge Beck. Just before this ford on the right hand side is an old quarry where in 1821 a quarryman discovered an entrance to a cave. This was explored by Dr. Buckland. The cave was about 100 yards long, the bones of 22 different kinds of animals were found which included wolves, elephants, ox, bears, deer, tiger, bison, reindeer, and the remains of 300 hyenas, also tools and weapons of Stone Age men. This was truly a most outstanding discovery.

Over the ford a little lane on the right leads us to St. Gregory's Minster tucked away in the dale, a secluded and very ancient monastery in the beautiful setting of cypress trees. There is a sundial over the timber gabled porch and another sundial inside the porch over the ancient doorway. It is rather a pity that the porch has been added, but it has given protection to what must certainly be the finest example of an Anglo-Saxon sundial. The date of this is about 1055. The dial is marked with eight hours of the Saxon's day and inscribed, "This is the day's Sun market at every tide". It is indeed very fascinating to decipher this clear inscription carved before the Conquest.

"ORM GAMAL'S SON BOUGHT ST. GREGORY'S MINSTER WHEN IT WAS ALL BROKEN AND FALLEN. HE LET IT BE MADE NEW FROM THE GROUND TO CHRIST AND ST. GREGORY IN EDWARD'S DAY AND IN TOSTI'S DAY THE EARL."

"HAWARTH ME WROUGHT BRAND THE PRIOR"

Gamal was murdered by Tosti (Tostig) the brother of Harold and was banished for this crime in 1065. Harold and Tostig fought at Stamford Bridge where Tostig was killed. Here in this sundial we have history recorded as it was recorded in the Bayeux Tapestry.

The inside of the Church has a very simple beauty. Some benches down the side of the walls are very ancient; in the very early days of the church there were no pews, the congregation assembled together, the infirm sat on the benches at the side. There are two ancient 7th century Anglo-Saxon coffins claimed as memorials to King Ethelwald of Deira and St. Cedd. This is doubtful, but both are certainly of great interest and design.

The stonework and woodwork are of simple beauty, one feels that this church has been a quiet retreat for a thousand years, history is recorded but has had very little impact.

Shaking myself out of this dream of history we leave the churchyard. For those who like to walk in this sylvan setting there is a footpath up to Sleightholmedale. Our route continues along the lane until it joins the A170 where we turn left and then after only a short distance right, back on to another unclassified road signposted Wombleton and Nunnington.

Wombleton is a village undisturbed, an ancient inn, cruck framed. Passing the old aerodrome of the forties we enter Nunnington across the splendid old bridge over the River Rye and immediately left we have another dream of history, Nunnington Hall, now a National Trust property, open on Wednesday and Sunday during the summer months. Here we have a fine example of an Old English Manor House, its history dating before the Conquest, a long history well described in the brochure available at the house. At one time it passed to the Grene family, Sir Thomas Parr of Kendal married Mathilda Grene and it was their daughter Catherine Parr who became Henry VIII's last wife. As we see the house today it is of two periods, Tudor and late Stuart. Much damage was done when it was occupied by the Parliamentary Army at the seige of Helmsley Castle. Lord Preston became owner in 1685, he was a great supporter of James II and was captured on a mission to the King in France. His valet disposed of incriminating documents by soaking them in the sea and eating them. Lord Preston imprisoned in the Tower was pardoned by King William as a result of the pleas of his small daughter to Queen Mary. He returned to Nunnington, built a house for his faithful servant and built the south front and east wing of the house. Above the balcony is the coat of arms of Lord Preston, this was done by the sculptor John Bunting in 1962 replacing the original.

Inside the house we enter the Stone Hall and visit the various rooms, the Smoking Room with a Constable painting of Hampstead Heath and an exquisite Sheraton writing table which opens out, the paper rack being lifted by counter weight, one could not wish to see finer craftsmanship.

Lord Preston's room has a painted ceiling displaying his coat of arms and those of his wife Lady Anne Howard. The Georgian Doll's House is of great interest to young visitors. Another fine Sheraton piece is here, a dressing table, the mirror so hinged as to go in any direction all neatly folding away for travelling. The Oak Hall looking on to the garden with a fine carved fireplace. Up the huge staircase 17th century tapestries adorn the walls and the Drawing Room looks over the garden which we were able to walk round before continuing our tour. The friendly way we were taken round the house made our visit most enjoyable.

The village of Nunnington is quite charming, rising from the River Rye on a slope towards Caulkleys Bank with almshouses and the 13th century Church of All Saints and St. James. We leave the village through avenues of sycamore trees and proceed to Hovingham.

This is a most charming village, stone cottages, village green, fine trees, a stream running through with fords and bridges. The old school has a most unusual oriel, and there is a fine late Georgian Inn. All Saints Church reconstructed 1860 with Anglo-Saxon Tower. Crowning all this is Hovingham Hall on the site of a Roman Villa. The Hall was planned and built about 1760 by Thomas Worsley, friend and Surveyor-General to George III. A group of beautiful lime trees leads us to the entrance to the Hall which is quite surprisingly a Riding School in the classical style. This must have been a great asset in the days of coach and horse. It reminds me of The Mews at the rear of Buckingham Palace. The accoustics of the Riding School are very good and many music festivals have been held here.

Occasionally The Hall is open for Charities, Tuscan columns and tapestried walls, rooms in different styles, Corinthian, Ionic and Doric, with lovely paintings and furniture. The garden front of the house is in the Palladian style the great lawn is the village cricket ground. This aspect of the house presents a fine prospect as one approaches Hovingham from the West. Hovingham Hall is a fine place in the best of Yorkshire traditions.

We leave Hovingham by the road B1257 to Stonegrave only about three miles away. On the slope facing south Holy Trinity Church appears to be 19th century but its interior and history prove it to be very ancient in fact one of a group of Saxon monasteries mentioned in a letter which Pope Paul I wrote in 757 to Eadbert, King of Northumbria, calling for the restoration of the monasteries of Stonegrave, Coxwold and Jarrow. After this interesting day of ancient historic churches and stately mansions we return as we came or join the A170 again at Helmsley.

Kirkdale — St. Gregory's Minster

Nunnington Hall

Hovingham — Bridge, Ford and Cottages

Hovingham — Entrance via Riding School

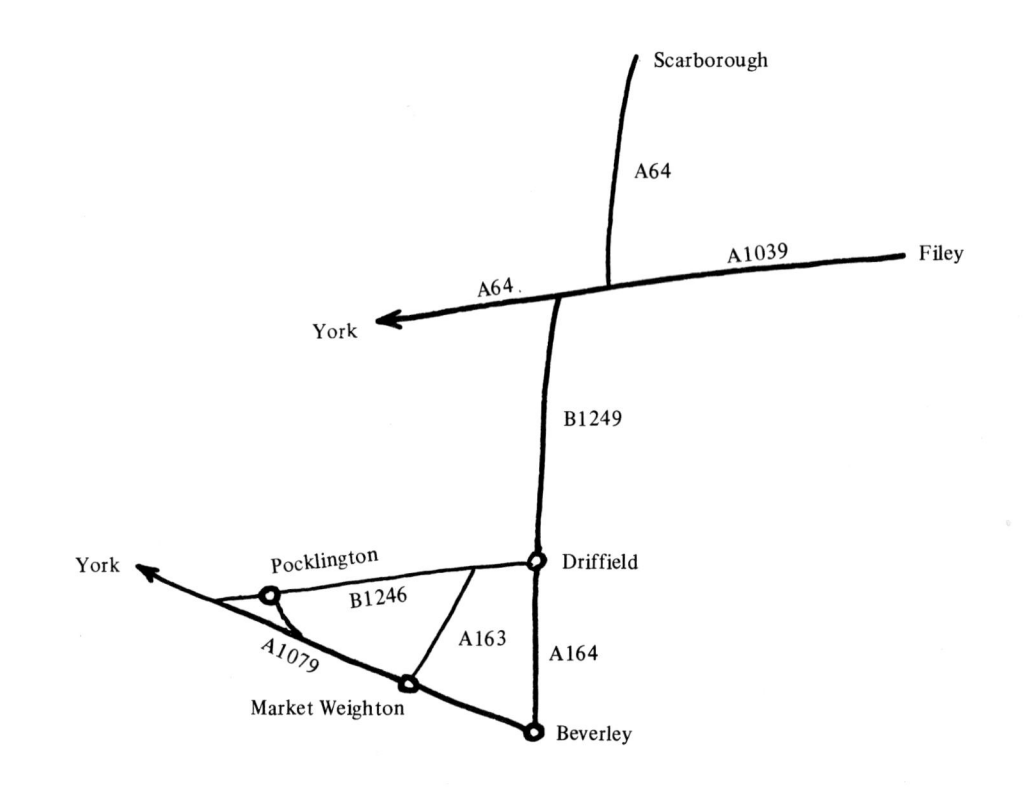

BEVERLEY & POCKLINGTON

We have been relaxing in quiet places, on moor, dale, coast and wold, but quiet places need not always be remote. My family and I have often relaxed in quiet places in the heart of large cities, even in London. Today we go over the wolds again to visit the beautiful county market town of Beverley, centre of the East Riding of Yorkshire.

The area round Beverley is rich, productive agricultural land, and the town has many interesting features, also thriving industrial and commercial enterprises. In my schooldays I was fascinated at the exciting sight of ships being launched broadside into the river, and just before I started to type this article from my notes such a launching was shown on television from Beverley.

There are well over 300 buildings scheduled as being of architectural or historic interest. I doubt if there is another town in the country with such a high proportion of dignified Georgian houses. St. Mary's Church is one of the most beautiful churches I have seen both externally and internally. The Minster is considered to be the finest example of Gothic architecture in Europe and Arthur Mee considered it to be one of the finest Gothic Churches in the world. So let us be tourists on our home ground and take a leisurely look at the quiet architectural and historic treasures of Beverley. Taking John Betjeman's advice we will walk.

We enter Beverley along New Walk which gives an immediate impression of excellent planning in the late 18th century, spacious and well proportioned buildings. The avenue of horsechestnut trees is most delightful in spring and autumn. The Sessions House is on the right. New Walk leads into North Bar Without, chestnut trees on the left and on the right a cobbled space between road and pavement where we park the car, the Georgian planners made adequate provision for parking coach and horse. If only planners today would take note. About us there are many fine examples of 18th century town houses, No. 62 was formerly the Beverley town house of the Sykes family of Sledmere and built about 1725.

Now we enter the older part of Beverley through the medieval North Bar, the last survivor of five ancient gateways, built of the old local narrow brick and dating from about 1409.

The East Riding double-decker buses were specially built to pass under this bar. We are now in **North**

Bar Within, quite a wide street again with Georgian houses on each side, on the left St. Mary's Manor. These houses have often beautiful interiors and this particular house has a circular dining room and another room with walnut panelling.

Next at the corner of North Bar Within and Hengate is St. Mary's Church, built of very pleasing coloured stone and quite like new, although the nave and tower were rebuilt in 1520 following the fall of the tower when people in the church were killed. The day before I wrote this account of our visit, I was talking about Beverley to some friends who told me that their daughter was confirmed at St. Mary's and that during the service some plaster dropped on them, startling them and rather distracting them from the ceremony. When I related the collapse of the tower they were glad they were not aware of this at the time!

Some of the church contains traces of the original Norman Church with an example of 13th century in the North Doorway. The chancel and aisles are chiefly 14th century, the West Window shows the transition from 14th to 15th century, whilst the Clerestory and East Window are 15th century.

Take note of the fine carving and the roof beautifully restored as it was in medieval times, blue with gold stars, the beams in bright colours and bosses in shining gold, the chancel roof with painted panels of English Kings. The medieval stalls are wonderfully carved. The most famous is the Minstrel's pillar in the north arcade attractively recording the benefactors of 1530.

There is much to relate but I have told enough I hope to inspire your visit if you have not yet been, and to revive your memory if you have already enjoyed its quiet beauty. So with prayerful thanks we leave and enter the first of the two market places. This, the Saturday market, is a square, very spacious, the central feature being a fine market cross in the form of an open shelter of a cupola supported by eight stone pillars adorned by eight stone urns and the Royal Arms of England, Queen Anne, the Arms of Beverley and of the Hotham and Warton families who contributed to its erection in 1711-4.

From the market square again with many Georgian buildings still retained we pass through Toll Gavel, the Guildhall dating from 1762 just to the right, then through to the Wednesday Market a smaller market place, then through Eastgate to The Minster.

Founded by John of Beverley as a monastery in the 8th century when he was Bishop of Hexham — later he became Bishop of York and was buried at Beverley in 721 — it was almost destroyed by the Danes in the 9th century but in the 10th century King Athelstan, following his victory at Brunanburgh, refounded the church as collegiate instead of monastic and granting the privilege of sanctuary.

Henry V came to the Minster to give thanks for victory at Agincourt. Henry VIII dissolved the college, and had it been still monastic it may never have survived. Queen Elizabeth I made it the Parish Church as it is today.

The story of the Minster is one of great interest, I can only tell a fraction and describe sufficient to arouse or renew your interest. The tower was built in 1051 but, after attempts to heighten it, collapsed in 1213, but rebuilding took place and as a result by 1260 the Eastern Arm in Early English Style was complete. The name reconstruction commenced in 1308 in Decorated Style, completion including the West Front and Towers, North Porch and East Window by 1420. The whole a beautiful composition.

The 68 choir stalls are original early 16th century, and the organ 1769. I cannot adequately describe the beautiful workmanship of masons, the carvings in stone and wood, the windows. The proportions of the interior, its light, the sculptured figures of Adam and Eve, Noah, Abraham, the twelve sons of Jacob, the New Testament figures, the Twelve Apostles, The Madonna, John the Baptist, Kings, Saints, The Percy Shrine, animals, flowers, The Frid Stool, the seat of the fugitives.

The Minster Clock is the only one in the world to strike bells in two towers, quarter chimes on ten bells in the North, the hours on Great John in the South tower. Time today goes too fast and how times have changed! The craftsmen who worked here were given the theme of their carving and carried out their craft to perfection, with satisfaction, often with humour portrayed in their work. If only today work could be done with the same contentment!

Time and again one can visit Beverley Minster and see and appreciate some detail missed before, one cannot absorb all at one visit. We give thanks for the creation of this beautiful House of God, for its architecture, art, music and spiritual survival. The least we can do in return is to make as generous a contribution as we can towards its maintenance.

So we wend our way back through the town of ancient trade, weaving, agriculture, tannery since 1359, shipbuilding, tailors and modern car components. The Borough retains its commons and enjoyable races. We used to like to watch the old saddler at work in his quaint shop but the last time we visited we learnt with sadness that this, another craftsman, had passed away.

After refreshment at The Beverley Arms and pleasant chat we continue our journey and today instead of returning by the same route I would like to take you back via Pocklington. We have been inside St. Mary's and The Minster, but to get the full benefit of the day out we must see some of Nature's beauty and the lilies at Burnby Hall, Pocklington, are at their best in July and August, so this is an opportunity not to be missed.

We leave Beverley via A1079 to Market Weighton, a small market town which has developed rapidly in recent years. About four miles out of Market Weighton we fork right along B1247. Burnby Hall Gardens are on this road on the outskirts of Pocklington. The Gardens are open April – September every afternoon. The collection of water lilies is reputed to be the finest in Europe, 5000 plants, over 50 varieties in two lakes. At the best season about 2000 lilies can be seen. The lakes were constructed by the late Major Stewart, originally for his own stretch of trout fishing; he was a keen fisherman, hunter and extensive traveller. During July and August The Stewart Collection of big game trophies is open to the public. Here we have tea before going to Pocklington, another small market town noted for its ancient grammar school founded in 1514 and now a public school. William Wilberforce was educated here and whilst still at school he wrote to a York newspaper protesting against the slave trade, and later secured their emancipation.

We leave Pocklington via B1246 through the very charming village of Warter with lovely thatched cottages, these wolds estates noted for barley and pedigree flocks of sheep.

Through Driffield the B1249 leads us back home after a very interesting day, fine Gothic and Georgian architecture, craftsmanship, gardens, rolling countryside, one of the granaries of England. The East Riding yields a rich harvest in so many ways.